The Pebble First Guide to

Dinosaurs

by Sally Lee

Consulting Editor: Gail Saunders-Smith, PhD

Consultant: Jack Horner, Curator of Paleontology
Museum of the Rockies
Bozeman, Montana

Capstone press®

Mankato, Minnesota

Pebble Books are published by Capstone Press,
151 Good Counsel Drive, P.O. Box 669, Mankato, Minnesota 56002.
www.capstonepress.com

Books published by Capstone Press are manufactured with paper
containing at least 10 percent post-consumer waste.

Library of Congress Cataloging-in-Publication Data
Lee, Sally.
    The Pebble first guide to dinosaurs / by Sally Lee.
    p. cm. (Pebble books. Pebble first guides)
    Includes bibliographical references and index.
    Summary: "A basic field guide format introduces 13 dinosaurs. Includes color
illustrations and range maps" — Provided by publisher.
    ISBN-13: 978-1-4296-3299-7 (library binding)
    ISBN-13: 978-1-4296-3858-6 (paperback)
    1. Dinosaurs — Juvenile literature. I. Title.
QE861.5.L45 2010
567.9 — dc22   2009004928

About Dinosaurs

The first dinosaurs lived about 230 million years ago. They have
been gone from the Earth for about 65 million years. No one
knows for sure what made the dinosaurs disappear. The lengths
given in this book measure each dinosaur from head to tip of tail.

Note to Parents and Teachers

The Pebble First Guides set supports science standards related to
life science. This book describes and illustrates 13 dinosaur species.
This book introduces early readers to subject-specific vocabulary
words, which are defined in the Glossary section. Early readers may
need assistance to read some words and to use the Table of Contents,
Glossary, Read More, Internet Sites, and Index sections of the book.

Table of Contents

Ankylosaurus

Say It: ang-kuh-loh-SORE-us

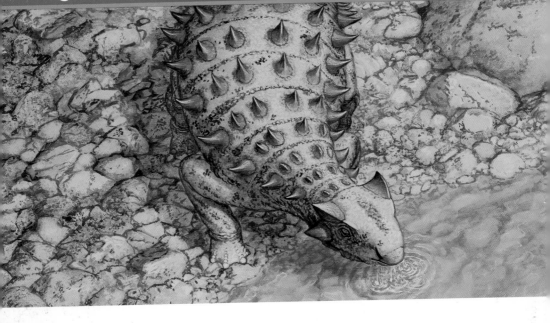

Length:	30 to 36 feet (9.1 to 11 meters)
Weight:	4 to 5 tons (3.6 to 4.5 metric tons)
Ate:	ferns and low-growing plants
Lived:	woodlands
Facts:	• body covered with armor • club at end of tail

Ankylosaurus Range

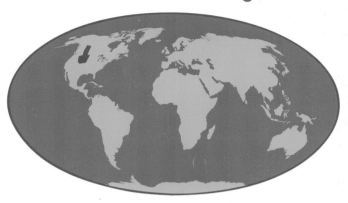

■ North America

Length:	70 to 90 feet (21 to 27 meters)
Weight:	33 to 35 tons (30 to 31.7 metric tons)
Ate:	ferns, conifers, gingko tree leaves
Lived:	woodlands
Facts:	• used to be called Brontosaurus
	• swallowed stones to help grind food in stomach

Apatosaurus Range

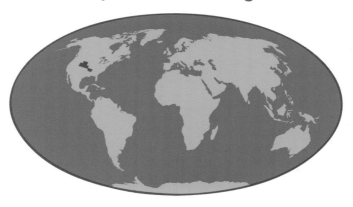

■ North America

Brachiosaurus

Say It: BRAY-kee-oh-sore-us

Length:	75 to 92 feet (23 to 28 meters)
Weight:	50 to 85 tons (45 to 77 metric tons)
Ate:	leaves from treetops
Lived:	woodlands
Facts:	• tallest dinosaur, stood 40 feet (12 meters) high • had nostrils on forehead

8

Brachiosaurus Range

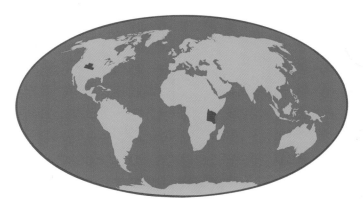

■ North America, Africa

Diplodocus

Length: 90 feet (27 meters)

Weight: 20 tons (18 metric tons)

Ate: ferns, conifers, gingko tree leaves

Lived: woodlands

Facts:
- its neck and tail made it one of the longest dinosaurs
- used tail as a whip

10

Diplodocus Range

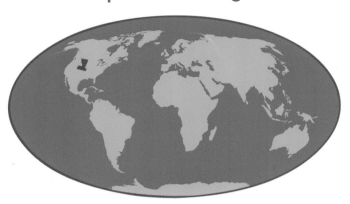

■ North America

Length: 30 to 43 feet (9.1 to 13 meters)

Weight: 4 to 5 tons (3.6 to 4.5 metric tons)

Ate: plants, gingko tree leaves, branches

Lived: marshes

Facts:
- thumb shaped like a sharp spike
- jaws moved sideways to grind food

Iguanodon Range

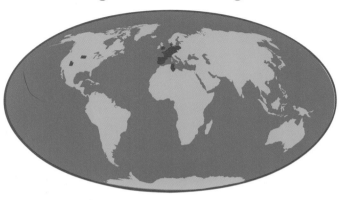

■ North America, Europe, Africa

Maiasaura

Length: 23 to 30 feet (7 to 9.1 meters)

Weight: 2 to 3 tons (1.8 to 2.7 metric tons)

Ate: leaves, twigs, fruit

Lived: plains

Facts:
- very fast-growing reptile
- name means "good mother lizard"

Maiasaura Range

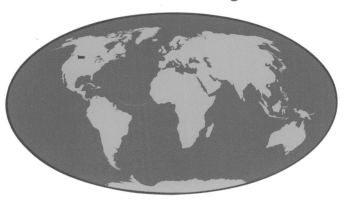

■ North America

Length:	30 feet (9.1 meters)
Weight:	2 tons (1.8 metric tons)
Ate:	ferns and low-growing plants
Lived:	woodlands
Facts:	• spikes on tail
	• plates of bone covered neck, back, and tail

Stegosaurus Range

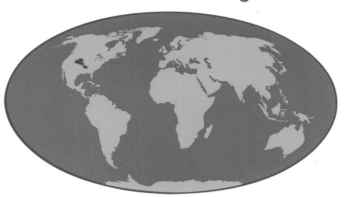

■ North America

Length: 25 to 30 feet (7.6 to 9.1 meters)

Weight: 6 to 8 tons (5.4 to 7.3 metric tons)

Ate: ferns and leaves of other plants

Lived: woodlands

Facts:
- two sharp horns above eyes and one on nose
- fan-shaped bone covered back of neck

18

Triceratops Range

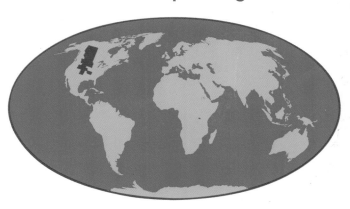

◼ North America

Allosaurus

Length: 36 to 45 feet (11 to 14 meters)

Weight: 2 to 3.6 tons (1.8 to 3.2 metric tons)

Ate: other dinosaurs

Lived: woodlands

Facts:
- low bump of bone in front of each eye
- 70 jagged teeth, each 3 inches (8 centimeters) long

Allosaurus Range

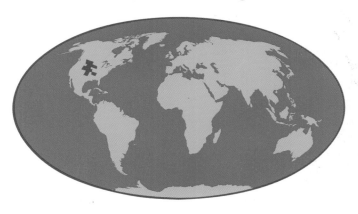

■ North America

Giganotosaurus   Say It: jig-uh-note-oh-SORE-us

Length: 43 to 48 feet (13 to 14.6 meters)

Weight: 8 tons (7.3 metric tons)

Ate: other dinosaurs

Lived: woodlands

Facts: • one of the biggest
          meat-eating dinosaurs
         • stood 15 feet (4.6 meters) tall

Giganotosaurus Range

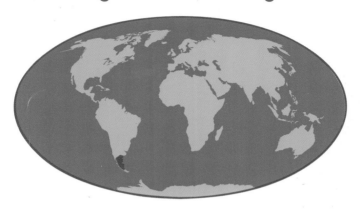

■ South America

Megalosaurus

Say It: meh-guh-low-SORE-us

Length:	30 feet (9.1 meters)
Weight:	1 ton (0.9 metric ton)
Ate:	other dinosaurs
Lived:	woodlands
Facts:	• hands had three fingers with sharp claws • first dinosaur fossil discovered

Megalosaurus Range

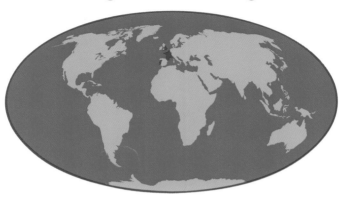

■ Europe

Length: 25 to 46 feet (7.6 to 14 meters)

Weight: 4.5 to 7 tons (4 to 6.4 metric tons)

Ate: other dinosaurs

Lived: woodlands

Facts:
- powerful, bone-crushing bite
- tiny front arms

Tyrannosaurus rex Range

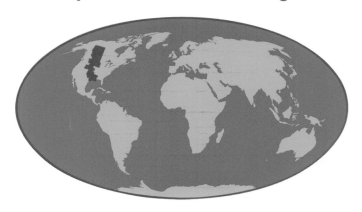

■ North America

Velociraptor

Say It: vuh-LAH-suh-rap-tuhr

Length:	6 feet (1.8 meters)
Weight:	33 pounds (15 kilograms)
Ate:	other dinosaurs and small animals
Lived:	deserts
Facts:	• fast runner • sharp, curved claw on each back foot

Velociraptor Range

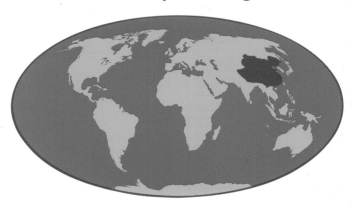

■ Asia

Glossary

armor — bones, scales, and skin that some animals have on their bodies for protection

conifer — trees that make cones; conifers are usually evergreen.

fossil — the remains or traces of an animal or a plant, preserved as rock

gingko — a tree with green, fan-shaped leaves

horn — a hard, bony permanent growth on the head of some animals

marsh — an area of wet, low land

plain — a large, flat area of land

plate — a flat, bony growth

reptile — a cold-blooded animal with a backbone; scales cover a reptile's body.

spike — a sharp, pointy object; dinosaurs used bony spikes for defense.

woodland — land that is covered by trees and shrubs

Read More

Brown, Charlotte Lewis. *The Day the Dinosaurs Died.* An I Can Read Book. New York: HarperCollins, 2006.

Kudlinski, Kathleen V. *Boy, Were We Wrong About Dinosaurs!* New York: Dutton Children's Books, 2005.

Internet Sites

FactHound offers a safe, fun way to find Internet sites related to this book. All of the sites on FactHound have been researched by our staff.

Here's all you do:

Visit *www.facthound.com*

FactHound will fetch the best sites for you!

Index

armor, 4
arms, 26
bodies, 4, 8, 10, 16,
    18, 20
claws, 24, 28
deserts, 28
eating, 6, 12
eyes, 18
feet, 28
fossils, 24
hands, 12, 24
height, 8, 22

horns, 18
jaws, 12
marshes, 12
name, 6, 14
necks, 10, 16, 18
nostrils, 8
plains, 14
spikes, 12, 16
tails, 4, 10, 16
teeth, 20
woodlands, 4, 6, 8, 10, 16,
    18, 20, 22, 24, 26

Grade: 1
Early-Intervention Level: 23

Editorial Credits
Katy Kudela, editor; Bobbi J. Wyss, book designer; Alison Thiele, set designer;
    Jo Miller, media researcher

Photo Credits
Capstone Publishers/James Field, cover (Allosaurus), cover (Ankylosaurus), cover
    (Tyrannosaurus rex), 4, 5, 9, 10, 12, 14, 15, 16, 20, 22, 26, 28, 29
Capstone Publishers/Steve Weston, cover (Triceratops), 6, 7, 11, 13, 17, 18, 19, 21, 23, 27
Jon Hughes, 24, 25
Photo Researchers Inc./Joe Tucciarone, 8